Indenture: Free to Live

Eunice E Frimpong

Clink
Street

London | New York

Published by Clink Street Publishing 2017

ISBN:
978-1-911525-98-1 - paperback
978-1-911525-99-8 - ebook

I would like to thank my parents in the Lord, Dr. Shadrach Ofosuware and Pastor Dorothy Ofosuware, for their faithfulness in living according to God's word; my father, Rev. Dr. Emmanuel Frimpong and mother, Mrs Alice Frimpong and sisters Grace Frimpong and Esther Frimpong, words cannot express their sure support and continual sacrifices; Regeneration Youth, under Pastor Segun Okunuga, at Freedom Centre International Church, for the first platform where I recited poems; Pastor Godfried Nsake, DNO and Tai-li Lee, all of whom sacrificed their time to share creative insights; Mr Possible Hackman and Mrs Abena Hackman, Bismark Nkansah and Fantah Seisay, for their great encouragement. It would be difficult to name all the people who have contributed to the production of this book, for your kind words, thank you so much.

For my father, my mother and my sisters.

A young
Leaf
Named
Lef,
Withering,
Fading,
Found other leaves on his tree lime green.

While he
Yellow,
Orange,
Brown,
A weakening hold on the branch,
Any minute now, he would fall to the ground and be
Swept away.

Ever
So
Afraid
He began to cry—
Foreknowledge
He'd soon
Die.

Ancient
Great
Grandmother
Green
Leaf told
Lef.

"Look all around
Other leaves,
Other trees.
Time leaves turn
Yellow, orange, brown.
We're green—
You're the renowned."

Abundant life:
I will have global firms.
Be a multi-millionaire, financier.
I will fund the word of God, to the distant shores.
Employ the unemployed and facilitate the poor.

Dominance expands, influences lands.

Yes I'm a Christian,
Can't live in lack.
God's my Provider and Height.
Not the other god in sight,
Money—dictator of life.

Man's true worth's not wealth.

Formed from dust,
Called through Christ,
God's restoring the Eden life.
Sons of God—Mature.
Take what's yours.

You've hurt me.
I think you should say:
"Sorry."
Then I'll say,
"Oh it's OK."

You've hurt me again.
I think you should say:
"Didn't know I hurt you,
Sorry."
Then I'll say, "Oh it's OK."

Days when you hurt me,
Repay, so the pain goes away.
Then say:
"Sorry."
And I'll say, "Oh it's OK."

How'll I control
What you do, what you say,
When you hurt me
And you don't say:
"Sorry."

How'll I forget,
Move on,
When I'm hurt, inside,
Unfair.
Give what I deserve, say:
"Sor…"

…you walk care free, what about me?

When I didn't know,
Couldn't show,
I was sorry—
Sins He forgave,
I can never repay.

You have hurt me.
But now I'm sorry.
Christ in me, I see
Forgiveness sets you free.

I'll touch,
Cultivate delight.
Allure,
Salivate the urge.
Awakening,
I'll enter in.

Floating…
Erupting…
Take it slow.
Delve into,
Flow through the unknown.

Explore you,
Intricate you.
Pursue, Into,
Crevices—you.
Two as one
Breakthrough.

Wife, arrive,
A multifarious mountain find,
Come.

Food cares?
You're force fed!

But he doesn't mean it,
Everything's changed.

I'm full
Tired every day.

Gained weight,
Can't curb intake—

Me,
It's me,
Hungering plates.
Vomiting cakes.
Love now hates—
Me.

See,
Addiction's Lord.
Surrender all.
God, Dominion install.

I hear them, my father, my mother. Next door.
The walls seem thick—aren't thick.
Words germinate to terminate love.
What's happening?
Please sleep.
Words.
It's dark outside.
Sleep please,
Death's in sight.

Heart pumps Hatred.
Lungs leak Lies.
Jealousy and Madness jostle for Mind.

No!
Vision.
Marriage.
Dead.

Go back,
Undo,
Don't. Want to
Can't. Bear it
Won't. Make it

I… do,
Honour father, mother
Blessing me.

Messed up.
Desperate.
Can't think.

Liberate me.

Grant normality.
Heal mentality.
Tired.

Laughing. Lost.

Why born?
No more.
Suicide.

Christian, wait!

Death has a glimpse
The cause you were born
And lives you'll restore
Fights to abort.

God,
Creator of body and mind
This healing is Thine.

Trust in, obey.
Love being The Way.

Narrow path, trained.
Power ablaze.

In God,
Spirit no limit.

I used to walk
A walk I knew to walk.

Those around—
Of the same mind.

Know God?
There was no God.

Only saw,
Love beyond human thought,
Peace defying storms.
Hope as good matured,
And the unseen formed.

I thought,
If I knew God
He'd be Lord over me

And so
Refused the word,
From believers living God's way.

I'd reiterate:
Jesus doesn't know me,
He doesn't love me,
He doesn't want me to know Him.

God's Word alive
Arrogance died
He's in charge
I'm His child.

www.ingramcontent.com/pod-product-compliance
Lightning Source LLC
Chambersburg PA
CBHW020038040426
42331CB00031B/984